THE
COLLEGE
COOKBOOK
FOR GUYS

SIMPLE AND DELICIOUS RECIPES TO FUEL YOUR STUDIES

ALETA A. BOLAND

TABLE OF CONTENTS

INTRODUCTION

About this cookbook

Are you a college student who is tired of eating just ramen noodles and take-out pizza? I do, however, have some good news to share with you! "the College cookbook for Guys: Simple and Delicious Recipes to Fuel Your Studies" is an excellent resource for honing your culinary skills.

This cookbook is designed just for young guys who need fast, cheap, and delicious meals to fuel their demanding schedules. This cookbook has something for everyone, whether you're a seasoned chef or a kitchen newcomer.

One of this cookbook's best qualities is that it covers all of the important meals of the day. Breakfast options include scrambled eggs with avocado toast, Greek yogurt parfait with granola and berries, a banana and peanut butter smoothie bowl, and oatmeal with apples and cinnamon. You may fill yourself before your morning classes without having to sacrifice sleep since all of these meals are quick and easy to make.

Among the full lunch options are grilled chicken Caesar salad, hummus and veggie wraps, tomato soup and grilled cheese sandwiches, and quinoa and black bean salad. These foods are ideal for bringing to class or eating at home during your break.

After a long day of studying, you'll find some substantial and scrumptious dinner options that are sure to satisfy your hunger. Among the dinner options are spaghetti with meat sauce, beef stir-fry with broccoli and rice, baked fish with lemon and herbs, and sweet potato and black bean chili. You won't have to spend hours in the kitchen after a long day of school since these recipes are not only delicious but also easy to prepare.

In addition to the main meals, this cookbook includes recipes for desserts, sides, and snacks. Snacks and sides include homemade trail mix, guacamole and chips, roasted sweet potato fries, and buffalo cauliflower bites. Baked apples with cinnamon and honey, apple crisp with vanilla ice cream, chocolate peanut butter energy balls, and chocolate chip banana bread are among the dessert choices.

"The college cookbook for guys" is an excellent resource for anybody trying to eat healthily on a budget while attending college. The recipes are easy to prepare, use affordable ingredients, and are sure to wow your friends and roommates. Why not give it a shot? Your taste buds will thank you!

Benefits of cooking your meals in college

Let's talk about the benefits of making your own meals while in college. I understand that eating at the dining hall or ordering takeout every day may be appealing, but there are several compelling reasons to spend some time in the kitchen.

First and foremost, cooking your own meals is often less costly than eating out. Cooking at home may be a great way to save money if you're on a tight budget, which, let's face it, the majority of college students are. You may plan your meals ahead of time, buy materials in bulk, and save food waste by just cooking what you need.

Furthermore, cooking your own meals may be considerably healthier than eating out often. When you make your food at home, you have more control over the components. Instead of processed foods and foods with high quantities of salt, sugar, and fat, choose fresh, whole ingredients. Furthermore, by preparing meals for yourself, you may ensure that your body receives the right balance of nutrients, which may boost your mood and academic performance.

Making your own food has the additional benefit of being a great stress reliever. Taking some time to focus on cooking and self-care may be a welcome respite from the demands of studying and socializing during the busy times of college. Cooking may also be a creative and amusing release, and you may discover a new hobby or passion.

Finally, cooking may be a great way to build a feeling of community and engagement. If your roommates or friends like cooking, you may make supper preparation a group endeavor. It is possible to share recipes, teach one another new skills, and connect through the satisfaction of producing something delicious together.

Having said that, making your own meals while at college may be a great way to save money, eat healthier, decrease stress, and develop community. Test it out and see how it goes.

Essential kitchen tools for college guys

A sharp chef's knife is the most important piece of equipment in any kitchen. It will make your prep work easier and faster, and it can be used for chopping, slicing, and dicing.

Cutting board: A sturdy cutting board is required for usage with your chef's knife. Select one that will not dull your knife and is easy to clean.

Several mixing bowls: Mixing bowls of various sizes are required for blending ingredients, marinating meat, and storing leftovers.

Measurement spoons and cups: Having a set of measuring cups and spoons on hand is vital for baking and cooking since exact measurements are required.

Blender or food processor: A blender or food processor isn't strictly essential, but it might come in handy for making smoothies, soups, sauces, and dips.

Avoid being caught without a can opener! It is a vital tool for opening canned items such as soup, beans, and veggies.

To flip and stir food while it cooks, you'll need some basic cooking tools like a spatula, slotted spoon, and tongs.

Pots and pans: You'll need at least one saucepan and one frying pan to create your dishes. Look for a nonstick surface to make cooking and cleaning easier.

A baking sheet is required for roasted vegetables, baked poultry, and other oven-cooked products.

Oven mitts: To protect your hands from burns, use a good pair of oven mitts.

Cooking in your apartment or dorm may be much easier and more enjoyable if you have these essential kitchen essentials on hand. Don't be afraid of cooking; with the appropriate tools and some practice, you'll be whipping up wonderful recipes in no time!

CHAPTER 1: BREAKFAST

Scrambled Eggs with Avocado Toast

Looking for a quick and delicious breakfast idea that will keep you energized throughout the day? Try making scrambled eggs with avocado toast! Here are the nutritional value, ingredients, and instructions you'll need:

Nutritional value

- Calories: 350
- Fat: 23g
- Carbohydrates: 18g
- Protein: 19g
- Fiber: 8g
- Sugar: 2g
- Sodium: 400mg

Ingredients

- 2 large eggs
- 1/2 ripe avocado
- 1 slice of whole wheat bread
- Salt and pepper to taste
- Butter or olive oil for cooking

Instructions

- ❖ Crack the eggs into a small bowl and whisk together with a fork until the yolks and whites are fully combined.
- ❖ Heat a small non-stick pan over medium heat and add a pat of butter or a drizzle of olive oil.
- ❖ Pour the eggs into the pan and use a spatula to scramble them as they cook. Cook until the eggs are just set but still slightly moist.

- ❖ While the eggs are cooking, toast the slice of bread in a toaster or in a separate pan until it's golden brown.
- ❖ Slice the avocado in half and remove the pit. Scoop out the flesh into a small bowl and mash it with a fork until it's slightly chunky.
- ❖ Spread the mashed avocado onto the toast and sprinkle with a pinch of salt and pepper.
- ❖ Serve the scrambled eggs on the side of the avocado toast and enjoy!

With just a few simple ingredients and steps, you'll have a nutritious and delicious breakfast that will give you the energy you need to tackle your day. Enjoy!

Greek Yogurt Parfait with Granola and Berries

Looking for a healthy and delicious breakfast or snack that is both satisfying and easy to make? Try this Greek Yogurt Parfait with Granola and Berries! Here are the nutritional value, ingredients, and instructions you'll need:

Nutritional value

- Calories: 320
- Protein: 20g
- Fat: 7g
- Carbohydrates: 46g
- Fiber: 7g
- Sugar: 22g

Ingredients

- 1 cup Greek yogurt (plain or vanilla)
- 1/2 cup granola
- 1/2 cup mixed berries (such as blueberries, raspberries, and strawberries)
- 1 tablespoon honey (optional)

Instructions

- ❖ In a bowl or glass, spoon in a layer of Greek yogurt.
- ❖ Add a layer of granola on top of the yogurt.
- ❖ Add a layer of mixed berries on top of the granola.
- ❖ Repeat the layers until the bowl or glass is full or all the ingredients are used.
- ❖ Drizzle with honey, if desired, for extra sweetness.
- ❖ Serve immediately and enjoy!

Banana and Peanut Butter Smoothie Bowl

Looking for a delicious and nutritious breakfast or snack that is both easy and satisfying? Try this banana and Peanut Butter Smoothie Bowl! Here are the nutritional value, ingredients, and instructions you'll need:

Nutritional value

- Calories: 400
- Protein: 16g
- Fat: 16g
- Carbohydrates: 53g
- Fiber: 10g
- Sugar: 24g

Ingredients

- 1 ripe banana
- 1/2 cup unsweetened almond milk (or milk of choice)
- 2 tablespoons peanut butter
- 1 tablespoon honey (optional)
- 1/4 teaspoon vanilla extract (optional)
- 1/2 cup ice cubes
- Toppings: sliced banana, granola, chia seeds, shredded coconut, chopped nuts, etc.

Instructions

- ❖ In a blender, add the ripe banana, almond milk, peanut butter, honey (if using), vanilla extract (if using), and ice cubes.
- ❖ Blend on high speed until smooth and creamy, scraping down the sides as needed.
- ❖ Pour the smoothie into a bowl.

❖ Add your favorite toppings, such as sliced banana, granola, chia seeds, shredded coconut, chopped nuts, or any other toppings you like.
❖ Serve immediately and enjoy!

Oatmeal with Apples and Cinnamon

Looking for a warm and comforting breakfast that is both healthy and delicious? Try this Oatmeal with Apples and Cinnamon! Here are the nutritional value, ingredients, and instructions you'll need:

Nutritional value

- Calories: 290

- Protein: 7g
- Fat: 5g
- Carbohydrates: 53g
- Fiber: 8g
- Sugar: 18g

Ingredients

- 1/2 cup rolled oats
- 1 cup water
- 1/2 cup unsweetened almond milk (or milk of choice)
- 1 apple, peeled, cored, and chopped
- 1/2 teaspoon ground cinnamon
- 1 tablespoon honey (optional)
- Toppings: chopped nuts, raisins, maple syrup, etc.

Instructions

- ❖ In a small pot, combine the rolled oats, water, and almond milk.
- ❖ Bring to a boil, then reduce heat to low and simmer for 5-7 minutes, stirring occasionally, until the oats are cooked and the mixture is creamy.
- ❖ Add the chopped apple, ground cinnamon, and honey (if using), and stir well to combine.
- ❖ Simmer for another 2-3 minutes, or until the apple is soft and the flavors are well blended.

CHAPTER 2: LUNCH

Grilled Chicken Caesar Salad

This Grilled Chicken Caesar Salad is a delicious and healthy meal that is easy to make and packed with protein and fiber. The grilled chicken adds a smoky and savory flavor to the salad, while the Parmesan cheese and croutons provide a delicious crunch. Plus, the homemade or store-bought Caesar dressing adds a tangy and creamy flavor that ties everything together. Give it a try and enjoy a delicious and nutritious meal that is perfect for lunch or dinner!

Nutritional Value

- Calories: 330
- Protein: 29g
- Fat: 19g
- Carbohydrates: 11g
- Fiber: 3g

Ingredients

- 2 boneless, skinless chicken breasts
- 2 teaspoons olive oil
- Salt and pepper, to taste
- 1 head romaine lettuce, washed and chopped
- 1/2 cup grated Parmesan cheese
- 1/2 cup croutons
- Caesar dressing (homemade or store-bought)

Instructions

- ❖ Preheat the grill to medium-high heat.
- ❖ Rub the chicken breasts with olive oil, and season with salt and pepper to taste.
- ❖ Grill the chicken for 5-6 minutes per side, or until cooked through.

❖ Remove the chicken from the grill and let it rest for a few minutes before slicing it into strips.
❖ In a large bowl, add the chopped romaine lettuce, grated Parmesan cheese, croutons, and sliced grilled chicken.
❖ Drizzle with Caesar dressing and toss to coat evenly.
❖ Serve immediately and enjoy!

Hummus and Veggie Wrap

This Hummus and Veggie Wrap is a delicious and healthy lunch option that is easy to make and packed with protein, fiber, and nutrients. The hummus provides a creamy and savory base for the wrap, while the chopped vegetables add a fresh and crunchy texture. Plus, the optional feta cheese adds a tangy and salty flavor that complements the vegetables perfectly. Give it a try and enjoy a delicious and nutritious meal that is perfect for a busy day!

Nutritional Value

- Calories: 240
- Protein: 7g
- Fat: 8g
- Carbohydrates: 36g
- Fiber: 8g

Ingredients

- 1 large whole wheat tortilla
- 2-3 tablespoons hummus
- 1/2 cup chopped vegetables (such as carrots, cucumbers, bell peppers, and tomatoes)
- 1/4 cup crumbled feta cheese (optional)

Instructions

- ❖ Spread the hummus evenly over the whole wheat tortilla.
- ❖ Add the chopped vegetables on top of the hummus.
- ❖ Sprinkle the crumbled feta cheese (if using) over the vegetables.
- ❖ Roll the tortilla tightly and slice it in half.
- ❖ Serve immediately or wrap it in foil or plastic wrap to take on-the-go.

Tomato Soup and Grilled Cheese Sandwich

Tomato Soup

Nutritional Value

- Calories: 120
- Protein: 3g
- Fat: 5g
- Carbohydrates: 16g

- Fiber: 3g

Ingredients

- 2 tablespoons olive oil
- 1 medium onion, diced
- 2 garlic cloves, minced
- 28-ounce can whole peeled tomatoes
- 1 1/2 cups chicken or vegetable broth
- 1/2 teaspoon dried basil
- Salt and pepper, to taste
- 1/4 cup heavy cream (optional)

Instructions

- ❖ Heat the olive oil in a large pot over medium heat. Add the diced onion and minced garlic and cook until the onion is soft and translucent, about 5-7 minutes.
- ❖ Add the whole peeled tomatoes (including their juice), chicken or vegetable broth, dried basil, salt, and pepper to the pot. Bring the mixture to a simmer and let it cook for 15-20 minutes.
- ❖ Use an immersion blender or transfer the soup to a blender to puree until smooth.
- ❖ If desired, stir in the heavy cream to make the soup extra creamy.
- ❖ Serve hot with a side of grilled cheese sandwich.

Grilled Cheese Sandwich

This classic combo of Tomato Soup and Grilled Cheese Sandwich is a comforting and delicious meal that is perfect for a chilly day. The tomato soup is packed with flavor from the onion, garlic, and basil, while the grilled cheese sandwich provides a crispy and cheesy complement. Give it a try and enjoy a tasty and satisfying meal!

Nutritional Value

- Calories: 320
- Protein: 16g
- Fat: 17g
- Carbohydrates: 28g
- Fiber: 1g

Ingredients

- 2 slices of bread
- 2 slices of cheese
- 1 tablespoon butter

Instructions

- ❖ Preheat a nonstick skillet over medium heat.
- ❖ Spread the butter on one side of each slice of bread.
- ❖ Place one slice of bread in the skillet, buttered side down.
- ❖ Place the cheese slices on top of the bread, then place the second slice of bread on top, buttered side up.
- ❖ Cook for 2-3 minutes on each side, until the bread is golden brown and the cheese is melted.
- ❖ Serve hot with a side of tomato soup.

Quinoa and Black Bean Salad

This quinoa and black bean salad is a healthy and delicious way to pack in some plant-based protein and fiber. The quinoa and black beans are a great source of vegetarian protein, while the avocado adds healthy fats and the red bell pepper and cilantro add a pop of color and flavor. This salad is perfect for meal prep or a quick and easy lunch or dinner. Enjoy!

Nutritional Value

- Calories: 240
- Protein: 10g
- Fat: 7g
- Carbohydrates: 36g
- Fiber: 9g

Ingredients

- 1 cup quinoa, uncooked
- 2 cups water or vegetable broth
- 1 can black beans, drained and rinsed
- 1 red bell pepper, chopped
- 1 small red onion, chopped
- 1 avocado, diced
- 1/4 cup cilantro, chopped
- 2 tablespoons lime juice
- 2 tablespoons olive oil
- Salt and pepper, to taste

Instructions

❖ Rinse the quinoa in a fine mesh strainer under running water. In a medium saucepan, bring the water or vegetable broth and quinoa to a boil. Reduce the heat to low, cover, and simmer for 15-20 minutes or until the liquid is absorbed and the quinoa is tender.

- ❖ In a large bowl, combine the cooked quinoa, black beans, red bell pepper, red onion, avocado, and cilantro.
- ❖ In a small bowl, whisk together the lime juice, olive oil, salt, and pepper. Pour the dressing over the salad and toss to combine.
- ❖ Serve immediately or refrigerate until ready to serve.

CHAPTER 3: DINNER

Spaghetti with Meat Sauce

Nutritional Value

- Calories: 400
- Protein: 24g
- Fat: 12g

- Carbohydrates: 48g
- Fiber: 6g

Ingredients

- 1 pound lean ground beef
- 1 can (28 oz.) crushed tomatoes
- 1 small onion, chopped
- 2 cloves garlic, minced
- 1 teaspoon dried basil
- 1 teaspoon dried oregano
- Salt and pepper, to taste
- 1 pound spaghetti

Instructions

- ❖ In a large saucepan, cook the ground beef over medium heat until browned. Drain any excess fat.
- ❖ Add the crushed tomatoes, onion, garlic, basil, oregano, salt, and pepper to the saucepan. Bring the mixture to a boil, then reduce the heat and simmer for 20-30 minutes.
- ❖ Meanwhile, cook the spaghetti according to the package directions until al dente.
- ❖ Serve the meat sauce over the cooked spaghetti.

Beef Stir Fry with Broccoli and Rice

Nutritional Value

- Calories: 450
- Protein: 30g
- Fat: 15g
- Carbohydrates: 50g
- Fiber: 4g

Ingredients

- 1 pound sirloin steak, sliced into thin strips
- 2 cups broccoli florets
- 1 red bell pepper, sliced
- 1 small onion, sliced
- 2 cloves garlic, minced
- 1 tablespoon vegetable oil
- Salt and pepper, to taste
- 2 cups cooked brown rice

Instructions

- ❖ In a large skillet, heat the vegetable oil over high heat. Add the sliced beef and cook for 2-3 minutes, or until browned.
- ❖ Add the broccoli, red bell pepper, onion, garlic, salt, and pepper to the skillet. Cook for an additional 5-7 minutes, or until the vegetables are tender.
- ❖ Serve the beef stir fry over cooked brown rice.

Baked Salmon with Lemon and Herbs

Nutritional Value

- Calories: 220
- Protein: 23g
- Fat: 13g
- Carbohydrates: 2g
- Fiber: 1g

Ingredients

- 4 salmon fillets
- 2 tablespoons olive oil
- 1 tablespoon lemon juice
- 1 teaspoon dried thyme
- 1 teaspoon dried rosemary
- Salt and pepper, to taste
- Lemon wedges, for serving

Instructions

❖ Preheat the oven to 400°F. Line a baking sheet with parchment paper.
❖ In a small bowl, whisk together the olive oil, lemon juice, thyme, rosemary, salt, and pepper.
❖ Brush the salmon fillets with the herb mixture and place them on the prepared baking sheet.
❖ Bake for 12-15 minutes, or until the salmon is cooked through and flakes easily with a fork.
❖ Serve with lemon wedges.

Sweet potato and black bean chili

This sweet potato and black bean chili is a hearty and healthy meal that is perfect for a cozy night in or for meal prepping for the week ahead. It's easy to make and can be customized to your liking with your choice of toppings. Enjoy!

Nutritional Value

- Calories: 300
- Protein: 12g
- Fat: 6g
- Carbohydrates: 50g
- Fiber: 13g
- Vitamin A: 184% of the Daily Value (DV)
- Vitamin C: 45% of the DV
- Iron: 20% of the DV
- Calcium: 12% of the DV

Ingredients

- 1 tablespoon olive oil
- 1 onion, chopped
- 3 cloves garlic, minced
- 1 red bell pepper, chopped
- 2 sweet potatoes, peeled and chopped
- 1 can (15 ounces) black beans, drained and rinsed
- 1 can (14.5 ounces) diced tomatoes, undrained
- 1 can (8 ounces) tomato sauce
- 1 tablespoon chili powder
- 1 teaspoon cumin
- 1/2 teaspoon smoked paprika
- Salt and pepper, to taste
- 2 cups vegetable broth

Instructions

- ❖ In a large pot or Dutch oven, heat the olive oil over medium heat. Add the onion and garlic and cook until the onion is translucent and the garlic is fragrant, about 3-4 minutes.
- ❖ Add the red bell pepper and sweet potatoes and cook for another 5-7 minutes, stirring occasionally, until the sweet potatoes are slightly softened.
- ❖ Add the black beans, diced tomatoes, tomato sauce, chili powder, cumin, smoked paprika, salt, and pepper, and stir well to combine.
- ❖ Pour in the vegetable broth and bring the chili to a boil. Reduce the heat and let the chili simmer for about 30-35 minutes, or until the sweet potatoes are tender and the flavors have melded together.
- ❖ Serve hot with your choice of toppings, such as shredded cheese, avocado, or sour cream.

CHAPTER 4: SNACKS AND SIDES

Homemade trail mix:

This homemade trail mix is a great option for a healthy and tasty snack that you can take with you wherever you go. The nuts and seeds provide protein and healthy fats, while the dried fruit adds natural sweetness and fiber. The dark chocolate chips also add a touch of indulgence and antioxidants. Plus, making your own trail mix allows you to customize it to your liking and avoid added sugars and preservatives found in store-bought options. Give it a try and enjoy!

Nutritional Value

- Serving size: 1/4 cup (about 30g)
- Calories: 140
- Total fat: 8g
- Saturated fat: 1g
- Sodium: 20mg
- Total carbohydrates: 14g
- Dietary fiber: 2g
- Sugars: 8g
- Protein: 4g

Ingredients

- 1 cup almonds
- 1 cup cashews
- 1/2 cup dried cranberries
- 1/2 cup raisins
- 1/2 cup dark chocolate chips
- 1/4 cup pumpkin seeds
- 1/4 cup sunflower seeds

Instructions

- ❖ Preheat the oven to 350°F (175°C).
- ❖ Spread the almonds and cashews on a baking sheet and bake for 10-12 minutes, or until lightly toasted.
- ❖ Let the nuts cool, then chop them roughly.
- ❖ In a large bowl, mix the toasted nuts, dried cranberries, raisins, dark chocolate chips, pumpkin seeds, and sunflower seeds.
- ❖ Stir well to combine.
- ❖ Store in an airtight container or portion into individual snack bags for a quick and easy snack on the go.

Guacamole and chips

Nutritional Value

- Calories: 200
- Total Fat: 14g
- Saturated Fat: 2g
- Sodium: 150mg
- Total Carbohydrates: 17g

- Fiber: 6g
- Sugar: 1g
- Protein: 3g

Ingredients

For the guacamole:

- 2 ripe avocados, peeled and pitted
- 1/2 small red onion, finely chopped
- 1 small jalapeño pepper, seeded and minced
- 2 tablespoons fresh lime juice
- 1/4 cup chopped fresh cilantro
- Salt and pepper to taste

For the chips:

- 10-12 corn tortillas
- Cooking spray
- Salt to taste

Instructions

❖ Preheat the oven to 375°F (190°C).
❖ To make the chips, cut the corn tortillas into small triangles and arrange them on a baking sheet. Spray the triangles with cooking spray and sprinkle with salt.
❖ Bake the chips in the preheated oven for 10-12 minutes, or until they are crispy and golden brown.

- ❖ While the chips are baking, make the guacamole. In a medium bowl, mash the avocados with a fork or a potato masher.
- ❖ Add the chopped red onion, minced jalapeño pepper, lime juice, and chopped cilantro to the bowl. Mix everything together until well combined.
- ❖ Season the guacamole with salt and pepper to taste.
- ❖ Serve the guacamole with the baked chips and enjoy!

Sweet Potato Fries

Roasted sweet potato fries are a great healthy alternative to regular fries. They're easy to make and packed with flavor, not to mention all the nutrients and vitamins that sweet potatoes offer.

Nutritional Value:

- Calories: 170

- Fat: 6g
- Carbohydrates: 27g
- Fiber: 4g
- Protein: 2g

Ingredients:

- 2 large sweet potatoes
- 2 tablespoons of olive oil
- 1/2 teaspoon of salt
- 1/2 teaspoon of pepper
- 1/2 teaspoon of paprika

Instructions:

- ❖ Preheat the oven to 400°F (200°C).
- ❖ Wash and peel the sweet potatoes, then cut them into 1/2-inch-thick fries.
- ❖ In a bowl, toss the sweet potato fries with olive oil, salt, pepper, and paprika until they're evenly coated.
- ❖ Spread the sweet potato fries in a single layer on a baking sheet lined with parchment paper.
- ❖ Roast in the oven for 20-25 minutes, or until they're crispy and golden brown on the outside.
- ❖ Remove from the oven and let cool for a few minutes before serving.

Buffalo cauliflower bites

Nutritional Value

- Servings: 4
- Calories per serving: 178
- Total Fat: 9g
- Saturated Fat: 2g
- Cholesterol: 3mg

- Sodium: 1303mg
- Total Carbohydrates: 22g
- Dietary Fiber: 6g
- Sugars: 6g
- Protein: 6g
- Vitamin D: 0%
- Calcium: 6%
- Iron: 8%
- Potassium: 7%

Ingredients

- 1 head of cauliflower
- 1/2 cup all-purpose flour
- 1/2 teaspoon garlic powder
- 1/4 teaspoon salt
- 1/4 teaspoon black pepper
- 1/2 cup water
- 1/2 cup buffalo sauce
- 2 tablespoons unsalted butter, melted
- 1 tablespoon honey
- Ranch or blue cheese dressing, for serving
- Chopped fresh parsley, for serving

Instructions

- ❖ Preheat your oven to 450°F (230°C).
- ❖ Line a baking sheet with parchment paper.

- ❖ Wash the cauliflower and chop it into bite-sized florets.
- ❖ In a bowl, whisk together the flour, garlic powder, salt, pepper, and water until smooth.
- ❖ Dip each cauliflower floret into the batter, letting the excess drip off, and place them on the prepared baking sheet.
- ❖ Bake for 20 minutes or until the cauliflower is golden and tender.
- ❖ While the cauliflower is baking, mix the buffalo sauce, melted butter, and honey in a bowl.
- ❖ Remove the cauliflower from the oven and toss it in the buffalo sauce mixture until well coated.
- ❖ Return the cauliflower to the baking sheet and bake for an additional 10 minutes or until crispy.
- ❖ Serve hot with ranch or blue cheese dressing and chopped fresh parsley on top. Enjoy!

CHAPTER 5: DESSERTS

Chocolate Chip Banana Bread

Nutritional Value

- Calories: 245
- Fat: 9g
- Carbohydrates: 38g

- Protein: 4g
- Fiber: 3g
- Sugar: 18g

Please note that these values may vary depending on the specific ingredients you use and the size of your servings.

Ingredients

- To make chocolate chip banana bread, you will need the following ingredients:
- 3 ripe bananas
- 1/3 cup melted butter
- 1 teaspoon baking soda
- Pinch of salt
- 3/4 cup sugar
- 1 large egg, beaten
- 1 teaspoon vanilla extract
- 1 1/2 cups all-purpose flour
- 1/2 cup chocolate chips

You may also choose to add chopped nuts, such as walnuts or pecans, to your banana bread if you like.

Instructions

- ❖ Preheat your oven to 350°F (175°C).
- ❖ Grease a 9x5 inch loaf pan.
- ❖ Mash the ripe bananas in a mixing bowl until smooth.

- Stir in the melted butter.
- Add baking soda and salt. Stir to combine.
- Mix in the sugar, beaten egg, and vanilla extract.
- Add the flour and stir until just combined. Do not overmix.
- Stir in the chocolate chips.
- Pour the batter into the prepared loaf pan and bake for 50-60 minutes or until a toothpick inserted into the center comes out clean.
- Let the bread cool for 10 minutes in the pan before removing it from the pan and placing it on a wire rack to cool completely.

That's it! Enjoy your delicious homemade chocolate chip banana bread!

Apple crisp with vanilla ice cream

Nutritional Value:

- Calories: 320
- Fat: 12g
- Carbohydrates: 54g
- Protein: 3g
- Fiber: 3g

- Sugar: 35g

Please note that this nutritional information may vary depending on the specific ingredients and brands used in the recipe.

Ingredients:

For the apple crisp:

- 6 cups of sliced apples (about 6-7 medium apples)
- 1 tablespoon of lemon juice
- 1/2 cup of granulated sugar
- 1/2 cup of all-purpose flour
- 1/2 cup of old-fashioned rolled oats
- 1/2 teaspoon of ground cinnamon
- 1/4 teaspoon of ground nutmeg
- 1/4 teaspoon of salt
- 1/2 cup of cold unsalted butter, cut into small pieces

For the vanilla ice cream:

- 1 cup of heavy cream
- 1 cup of whole milk
- 1/2 cup of granulated sugar
- 1 teaspoon of vanilla extract

Instructions:

For the apple crisp:

- ❖ Preheat your oven to 375°F (190°C).
- ❖ In a large bowl, toss the sliced apples with the lemon juice.
- ❖ In a separate bowl, mix together the sugar, flour, oats, cinnamon, nutmeg, and salt.
- ❖ Add the butter to the dry mixture and use a pastry cutter or your hands to mix it in until the mixture becomes crumbly.
- ❖ Pour the crumb mixture over the sliced apples and stir until the apples are evenly coated.
- ❖ Transfer the apple mixture to a 9-inch baking dish and bake for 45-50 minutes or until the top is golden brown and the apples are tender.

For the vanilla ice cream:

- ❖ In a medium saucepan, heat the heavy cream, whole milk, and sugar over medium heat until the sugar has dissolved.
- ❖ Remove the pan from the heat and stir in the vanilla extract.
- ❖ Pour the mixture into a large container and refrigerate until it has cooled completely.
- ❖ Pour the cooled mixture into an ice cream maker and churn according to the manufacturer's instructions.
- ❖ Transfer the ice cream to a container and freeze for at least 2 hours before serving.

To serve:

Spoon the warm apple crisp into bowls and top with a scoop of vanilla ice cream.

Enjoy!

Chocolate peanut butter energy balls

These chocolate peanut butter energy balls are a delicious and healthy snack that you can enjoy on the go or as a midday pick-me-up. They're packed with protein and fiber, which will keep you feeling full and energized for longer. Plus, they're super easy to make and can be customized to your liking - try adding in some shredded coconut or swapping out the peanut butter for almond butter for a fun twist!

Nutritional Value

- Serving size: 1 energy ball
- Calories: 97
- Total fat: 5g
- Saturated fat: 1g
- Carbohydrates: 11g
- Fiber: 2g
- Sugars: 6g
- Protein: 4g

Ingredients

- 1 cup rolled oats
- 1/2 cup creamy peanut butter
- 1/4 cup honey
- 1/4 cup ground flaxseed
- 1/4 cup mini chocolate chips
- 1/4 cup chopped roasted salted peanuts
- 1 teaspoon vanilla extract

Instructions

- ❖ In a large mixing bowl, combine the oats, peanut butter, honey, flaxseed, chocolate chips, peanuts, and vanilla extract.

- ❖ Stir until all the ingredients are well combined and the mixture is sticky.
- ❖ Using your hands, roll the mixture into small balls, about 1 inch in diameter.
- ❖ Place the energy balls onto a baking sheet lined with parchment paper.
- ❖ Refrigerate the energy balls for at least 30 minutes, or until they are firm.
- ❖ Once firm, the energy balls can be stored in an airtight container in the refrigerator for up to 1 week.

Baked apples with cinnamon and honey

These baked apples with cinnamon and honey are a delicious and healthy dessert that's perfect for fall or any time of year. They are low in calories and packed with fiber, making them a great way to satisfy your sweet tooth without derailing your diet. Plus, the combination of warm cinnamon and sweet honey is sure to hit the spot!

Nutritional Value

- Calories: 135 kcal
- Fat: 0.4 g
- Carbohydrates: 35 g
- Fiber: 6 g
- Protein: 0.5 g

Ingredients

- 4 apples
- 1 tablespoon cinnamon
- 1 tablespoon honey
- 1 tablespoon coconut oil

Instructions

❖ Preheat your oven to 375°F (190°C).
❖ Cut the apples in half and remove the core with a spoon or apple corer. Place them in a baking dish with the skin-side down.
❖ In a small bowl, mix together the cinnamon and honey. Spoon the mixture evenly over the apples.
❖ Melt the coconut oil in the microwave or on the stovetop and drizzle it over the apples.
❖ Bake the apples for 20-25 minutes, or until they are tender and golden brown.
❖ Serve hot, either on their own or with a scoop of vanilla ice cream.

CONCLUSION

Cooking for oneself is an important life skill that every college guy should acquire. Not only does it save money, but it also promotes healthy eating habits and can be a great way to destress from a long day of studying. With the right tools and recipes, cooking can be a fun and enjoyable activity.

When it comes to essential kitchen tools, it's important to invest in items that will last and make cooking easier. A good set of knives, cutting board, pots and pans, measuring cups and spoons, and a blender or food processor are all worthwhile investments. Additionally, having basic pantry staples such as oils, spices, and grains on hand can make meal prep quick and easy.

There are so many simple and delicious recipes that college guys can make in their own kitchen. From quick and easy breakfasts like Greek yogurt parfait with granola and berries or oatmeal with apples and cinnamon, to more substantial meals like grilled chicken Caesar salad or beef stir fry with broccoli and rice, there's something for every taste preference. And for those with a sweet tooth, chocolate chip banana bread or baked apples with cinnamon and honey are great dessert options.

Cooking for oneself in college is a valuable life skill that can lead to a healthier and more enjoyable lifestyle. By investing in essential kitchen tools, stocking up on pantry staples, and trying out new recipes, college guys can become confident and proficient cooks in no time.

Made in the USA
Coppell, TX
15 December 2024

42384188R00039